Fundamental
HOCKEY

Coach Mike Foley and the following athletes were photographed for this book:
Mike Brown,
Mark Foley,
Michael Kozlowski,
Tim McManus,
Heather Murphy,
Marisa Pettiford,
Robb Pottle,
Travis Prunty,
Tony Rocha,
Chad Taylor.

Fundamental
HOCKEY

Mike Foley

Photographs by Andy King

Lerner Publications Company ● Minneapolis

To Elsie, for her untiring support, love, and inspiration

Library of Congress Cataloging-in-Publication Data

Foley, Mike.
  Fundamental hockey/Mike Foley ; photographs by Andy King.
    p. cm.—(Fundamental sports)
  Includes bibliographical references and index.
  Summary: An introduction to the sport of ice hockey, including its history, equipment, techniques, and variations.
  ISBN: 0-8225-3456-8 (alk. paper)
    1. Hockey—Juvenile literature. [1. Hockey.] I. King, Andy, ill. II. Title. III. Series.
GV847.25.F65 1995
796.962—dc20   95-7077

Manufactured in the United States of America

1 2 3 4 5 6 – HP – 01 00 99 98 97 96

The Fundamental Sports series was conceptualized by editor Julie Jensen, designed by graphic artist Michael Tacheny, and composed on a Macintosh computer by Robert Mauzy.

Photo Acknowledgments
Photographs reproduced with permission of: pp. 7, 8 National Archives of Canada (neg. # C1007, C81683); p. 9, ALLSPORT/Steve Powell; p. 11, Courtesy of the Los Angeles Kings; p. 42, Courtesy of the Las Vegas Thunder; pp. 70, 73, ALLSPORT/Jed Jacobsohn; p. 71, Mick Fletten; p. 72, Ringette Canada; p. 73, Sledge Hockey Canada.
All diagrams by Laura Westlund.

Contents

Chapter 1

How This Sport Got Started

Unlike soccer, baseball, football, and golf, hockey is played on ice. But hockey wasn't always an ice game. It began as a sport called bandy, or field hockey, that was played on grass.

Hockey was played on ice in England as early as the 1820s and in Canada in the late 1800s. In 1890 the Ontario Hockey Association was founded. Hockey began in the United States with a game between teams from Yale and Johns Hopkins Universities in 1893.

In 1904 the first professional hockey league, the International Hockey League, was formed. Teams from both Canada and the United States played in it. The league lasted only three years, however, because the small rinks where the games were played couldn't generate enough money to keep the league in business.

The First Stanley Cup

Lord Stanley of Preston, the Governor General of Canada in 1893, presented an award to the champion of the Amateur Hockey Association of Canada. That first Stanley Cup trophy, named in honor of Lord Stanley, was given to the Montreal Amateur Athletic Association. The Stanley Cup has been awarded every year since as a symbol of hockey supremacy. It is still awarded to the championship team of the National Hockey League.

Frozen ponds and outdoor rinks offered early hockey players places to play. This photograph was taken in about 1880 at McGill University in Montreal, Quebec.

A few other professional leagues were soon organized. In 1917 two leagues—the National Hockey Association and the Pacific Coast League—combined to form the National Hockey League (NHL). At first, the NHL included only teams from Canada. The Boston Bruins joined the league in 1924, however, and other U.S. teams soon followed.

More than a million men and women in the United States, Canada, Europe, and throughout the world play hockey. Boys and girls, ages 4–18, in the United States play in community hockey associations. There are beginner programs (called Initiation Programs) for youngsters 4 to 8 years old.

There are also competitive programs for termites (ages 5 and 6), mites (7 and 8), squirts (9 and 10), peewees (11 and 12), bantams (13 and 14), midgets (15 and 16), and junior golds (17 and 18). Check with your local recreation center to see what's available at your age level in your community.

There are also many high school teams and some Junior A and Junior B teams. Some colleges and universities have competitive intercollegiate teams. Colleges also have club teams, which are organized and run by the players rather than by the schools. Intramural ice hockey is also popular. Some colleges register as many as 50 teams!

Teams from many countries compete for the bronze, silver, and gold medals in the Olympic Games. The top level of play, however, is in the NHL. These professional players have tremendous skills. Thousands of fans fill huge arenas across Canada and the United States to watch these athletes compete. Every spring, millions of people watch the final play-off games to see which team will win the Stanley Cup Championship, the symbol of hockey supremacy.

An Olympic Miracle!

We all like stories with happy endings, especially when it's the underdog who wins. Such was the case in the hockey competition at the 1980 Winter Olympics at Lake Placid, New York.

The United States hadn't won a gold medal in ice hockey since 1960. The competition had been dominated by Canada and the Soviet Union. When the Olympic torch was lit in 1980, however, Coach Herb Brooks had plans for a different ending for Team USA. His team was seeded seventh going into the Olympics. No one thought the Americans would win a medal of any kind. No one, that is, except Coach Brooks.

While the other teams in the medal round had rosters filled with older, more experienced players, Coach Brooks had the youngest team in Olympic history. In the early games, his college kids managed to surprise some of the other teams. Almost before anyone realized what was happening, the young Americans were facing off against the powerful Soviet Union team in the semifinal game. The Lake Placid fire marshal must have stayed away, because the arena was filled well beyond capacity. Every corner and aisle was jammed with excited fans.

Midway through the third period, the score was tied 3-3. Thousands of fans in the arena and millions gathered around their television sets at home wondered, "What if . . . ?" Hundreds of red, white, and blue flags waved in the arena as chants of "U.S.A. . . . U.S.A. . . . U.S.A. . . . " filled the building.

Then it happened. Mike Eruzione, a youngster from Winthrop, Massachusetts, broke through the slot and fired the shot heard around the world as he beat Soviet goaltender Vladimir Myshkin for a 4-3 lead. Hockey fans, casual spectators, and even people who had never before seen a game celebrated. As the final seconds of the game ticked away, the television play-by-play announcer asked, "Do you believe in miracles . . . ?"

Led by goaltender Jim Craig, Team USA hung on for the stunning victory. The United States then defeated Finland, 4-2, in the championship to win the 1980 gold medal.

Chapter 2

BASICS

Ice hockey is the fastest sport in the world. Teams of six players, all on skates, race up and down the ice. The players use long, slender sticks to hit the hard rubber **puck** at speeds of more than 100 miles an hour. Players even make substitutions without waiting for the game to stop. That's fast!

The object of all this effort is to put the puck, which is 3 inches in diameter and 1 inch thick, into the opponent's **goal**. Each time a team does this, it scores a point, which is also called a goal. The team with the most points at the end wins the game. A game is divided into three periods, with short intermissions between periods. Merely slide a small puck into a huge net and you score a point? It may sound easy, but it isn't.

The Great One's Goof-up

Wayne Gretzky is one of hockey's greatest players of all time. In fact, his nickname is "The Great One." After leading the Edmonton Oilers to several Stanley Cup Championships, he continues as professional hockey's all-time leading scorer while playing for the Los Angeles Kings. He knows a lot about goals!

Wayne tells the story in his autobiography of how, when he was 13 years old, he and his dad decided to build a pair of regulation nets. They worked for days, constructing them in their basement. Finally, the day came to bring the nets outside.

Excitement reigned as they struggled to lift and carry the goal frames. There was one problem, however, and it was a serious one. The nets were too large to fit through the basement door. They had to be cut into three pieces!

11

The Rink

In cold climates, hockey can be played outdoors on natural ice, such as frozen lakes and ponds. More often, though, hockey is played indoors on artificial ice. Large refrigeration systems keep the playing surface frozen.

A typical **rink** is 200 feet long and 85 feet wide. It has curved corners and is surrounded by **boards** that are 42 inches high. Strong plastic extends another 5 to 8 feet above the boards. The boards and plastic protect spectators and keep the puck in the rink.

The rink is divided in half by the **red line,** also called the center line. In the middle of the center line is the center **face-off** circle. This is where play begins at the start of each period and after a goal has been scored. Short blue lines around the face-off circles indicate where players are supposed to stand for a face-off.

At each end of the rink is a red **goal line** that stretches across the rink. At the middle of the goal line is a goal. A hockey goal is a steel frame with heavy nylon mesh netting stretching between the goal posts and crossbar. The goalmouth is 6 feet wide by 4 feet high. A 6-foot light blue semicircle in front of the goal is outlined in red. This area is the **goal crease.** Players can't enter their opponent's goal crease unless the puck is already there.

Two **blue lines** divide the area between the goal lines into three zones. The zone in the middle of the rink is called the **neutral zone.** In addition to the center face-off circle, there are four face-off spots in the neutral zone. A team's goal is in its **defending zone.**

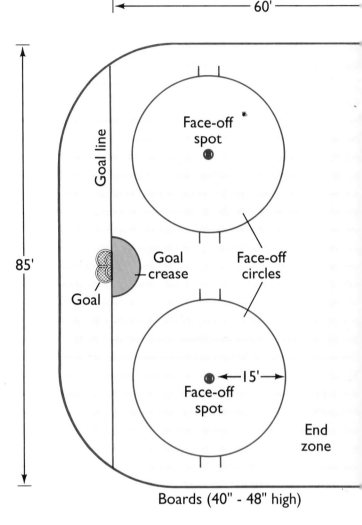

The Rink

The other end zone is that team's **attacking zone** or offensive zone. Each end zone is 60 feet long and has two face-off circles.

Near center ice there is a **referee's crease** and the door to the **penalty box.** Players sit in the penalty box when they have broken a rule of the game. The other players and coaches sit on team benches, which are also between the blue lines at center ice.

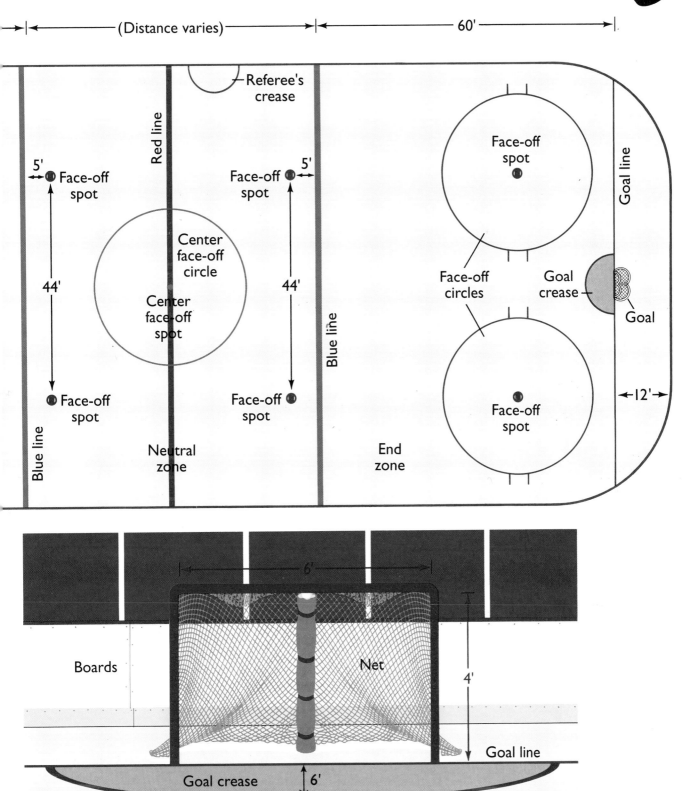

(Distance varies)   60'

Referee's crease

Red line

5'   Face-off spot

5'   Face-off spot

Face-off spot

Goal line

Center face-off circle

44'

Center face-off spot

44'

Blue line

Face-off circles

Goal crease

Goal

Blue line

Face-off spot

Face-off spot

12'

Neutral zone

End zone

Face-off spot

6'

Boards

Net

4'

Goal line

Goal crease

6'

The Goal

The Hockey Stick

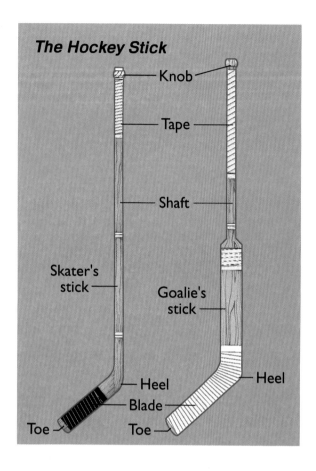

Knob

Tape

Shaft

Skater's stick

Goalie's stick

Heel

Heel

Blade

Toe

Toe

Lies of Sticks

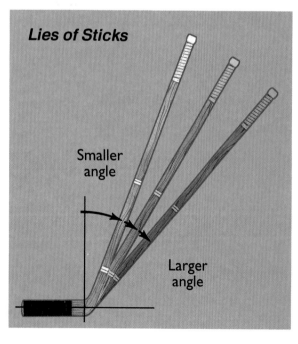

Smaller angle

Larger angle

The Equipment

With players skating so fast and shooting the puck at high speeds, most hockey equipment is designed to protect the players. Hockey skates have steel blades and a rigid boot that supports the ankle and protects the entire foot. A player's legs are protected by shin pads and padded pants called breezers. Elbow pads and shoulder pads protect the arms and shoulders, and protective gloves cover the wrists and hands. Each player also wears a helmet with a face mask and mouth guard.

One important piece of equipment isn't for protection—the hockey stick! A player holds the stick by its shaft and shoots the puck with the blade. The angle at which the blade meets the shaft is called the **lie** of the stick. The smaller the angle, the easier it is to control the puck when it is close to you. But with a larger angle, you can control the puck in a bigger area.

Most sticks are made entirely of wood, usually ash, but some have an aluminum shaft with a replaceable wooden blade. Sticks are designated as either right or left. If you are a right shooter, you place your right hand one-third of the way down the shaft and hold the end of the stick with your left hand. If you are a left shooter, you do the opposite.

Five of the six players on a hockey team use all of this equipment. Those five skaters move all over the rink. One player, however, needs different equipment. That player is the **goaltender**, or goalie, who must stay near the goal. The goalie tries to block the blistering shots being fired by the opposing team and prevent the puck from entering his or her team's goal. Shots that the goalie prevents from scoring are called **saves**. Saves and goals are called **shots on goal**.

Goaltenders wear skates with extra padding, large leather blocker pads on their legs, breezers, a chest protector, elbow pads, and arm and shoulder pads. The goalie also wears a blocking glove and holds the stick with that hand. The goaltender catches pucks with a catching glove on the other hand. A face mask and mouth guard complete the goaltender's protective equipment.

Before stepping into the goal crease, however, a goalie needs a stick. The goaltender's stick has a shaft that is narrow at the top. The shaft widens into a paddle at the blade to give a goalie more surface area with which to stop the puck.

Now that the equipment is taken care of, let's observe what hockey players do at practice.

Stretching and Warm-up

As soon as practice starts, the players stretch their upper and lower body muscles. This is done very gradually with slow movements. After several minutes, the players begin skating at half speed, then three-quarters, and finally full speed to complete their warm-up.

Power Skating

Next, the players sprint the length of the rink, practicing their **power skating**. Their coach tells them to keep their knees bent, hips low, chins up, and chests out for the best balance.

Travis is a good skater. Notice that his right skate is turned outward for the power thrust. As he pushes off his right skate, Travis's left skate is pointed straight ahead in the glide position. After the power thrust or push, Travis's right leg is fully extended and his left knee remains well bent for the glide. Then, he brings his right skate up to the heel of his left skate. He keeps his right skate low and close to the ice during this recovery. Travis's right skate then becomes the glide blade, and his left skate becomes the thrust or push blade. He alternates these strides from the right and left sides to move up the ice very rapidly.

After several forward sprints, the players practice backward skating. The coach reminds them to keep their knees well bent, hips low, and their chins up and chests out for good balance and form.

Mike is the best backward skater on his team. Notice how his feet are about shoulder width apart. He begins skating backward by pushing off the inside edge of his right skate and then gliding on his left skate. Mike alternates sides, pushing and gliding. In just a few seconds he has skated all the way to the other end of the rink. Coach reminds all the skaters that for backward skating, they use the inside edge and the front of their skate blades for the power thrust or push.

Crossovers

Skating turns are very important. Players must be able to make turns to their right and left sides while skating forward or backward.

For backward turns, you can use the **crossover** stride Mike is demonstrating below. Maintain good skating form, with your knees bent, hips low, chest out, and chin up for good balance. If you are turning to your left side, ride the outside edge of your left skate. Then, pick up your right skate and cross it over your left foot. Place your left skate back on your left side to complete one stride. As you repeat this sequence, you will gain speed and agility on your backward turns.

Forward crossovers are used, of course, when skating forward. If you are turning toward your left side, as Travis is doing, keep your knees well bent and ride the outside edge of your left skate. Push off the inside edge of your right skate, and then bring it all the way over your left foot. Place your left skate back on your left side to complete one forward crossover stride.

Travis does well on forward crossovers to his left, but he doesn't do nearly as well when going to his right. He knows that his coach is correct when he says that to be a complete hockey player, Travis must be able to execute all of the skills to both his right and left sides. So he practices forward crossovers to his right a little more.

Puck Carrying

When the players see their coach drop 20 pucks on the ice, they know it's time to practice **puck carrying**. About half of the players are right shooters and half are left shooters. The right shooters have their left hand at the top, or knob, of the stick, and their right hand about one-third of the way down the shaft. Left shooters, like Mark, do the opposite, with their right hand at the top and their left hand lower on the stick's shaft. A right shooter's **forehand** side is his or her right side. A left shooter's left side is his or her forehand side. The side that isn't the forehand side is the shooter's **backhand** side.

Coach blows his whistle, and each skater holds the stick only at the top while releasing his or her bottom hand. Keeping the puck on the forehand side of the blade, each skater pushes his or her puck up the ice using the forehand carry.

After several trips up the ice, the players turn their stick blades to their backhand sides to practice the backhand carry. These two carries are the fastest ways to push the puck up the rink when you are the puck carrier. Their coach reminds the skaters to keep their heads up while carrying the puck so that they can see their teammates and opponents.

Forehand carry

Backhand carry

Ready position

Stickhandling

Next, the players practice their **stick-handling**. First they assume the ready position, with their skates straight ahead and at shoulder width, knees bent, heads up, and arms out away from their bodies. Chad is in the ready position at left.

To execute the side-to-side dribble, Travis taps the puck back and forth across his body. He starts slowly and moves faster as he improves.

For the forward-and-back dribble, Travis turns his stick to the side. He pushes the puck away from his skates, and then he brings it back.

Forward-and-back dribble (photo above and bottom two photos on next page)

Side-to-side dribble: Travis brings the puck from his right side, across his body, to his left.

For the diagonal dribble, Travis moves the puck from the right to the left side, but in a diagonal direction rather than straight across his body.

All three dribbles are important when you are stickhandling. The best stick-handlers combine all three patterns. By moving the puck quickly, they can control the puck and confuse even the best defenders.

Goaltending

After several minutes of stickhandling, Robb, a goalie, skates to the goal crease and takes his position there. First, Robb takes the basic stance, with his feet together, his knees and waist bent, and his chin and shoulders up for balance. He has his catching glove open and out to his side, ready to catch pucks that are shot to the glove side of his body. Robb holds his stick in his blocking glove. He uses the blocking glove to deflect high shots to his stick side.

From the basic stance, Robb can also drop to the **V save** position. His knees are together with his skates wide apart, forming an upside-down V with his legs.

The catching and blocking moves shown below are called **glove saves.** Robb's stick blade is flat on the ice, and he stays square to the puck by following its movement on the rink. Goalies try to return to the basic stance as quickly as possible after making a save.

Basic stance

● Skate Save

Robb knows many different ways to make a save. To make a **skate save**, above, Robb moves his skate blade in an arc to stop shots that are on the ice, not in the air. He practices doing this to both his left and right.

● Stick Save

He can also stop low shots with his stick blade, as he is doing in the photograph at left. This is called a **stick save**. For shots in the range of four inches off the ice to knee height, Robb kicks out his leg to make a **pad save**.

● *Deck Save*

Another important goaltending move is the **deck save,** or stacked pads slide save. When Robb does a deck save to his stick side, he slides on that side and stretches out his arm and stick as far as possible. He puts one leg on top of the other and puts his catching glove arm on top. He can do the same save to the other side.

As a goaltender, you should try to stay up on your skates as much as possible. But as you can see, the deck save allows your body to cover almost all of the lower net. This makes it an effective save when an opposing puck carrier comes at you all alone and tries to fake to the right or left side.

● Rebounds

Sometimes during a game Robb catches the puck and holds it until the referee blows his or her whistle. Other times, when Robb is down on the ice, he keeps the puck under his body until play is stopped. This is called freezing the puck.

But many times, after Robb has made a save, the puck bounces off his equipment and onto the ice in front of the net. A loose puck in this situation is called a **rebound**. Rebounds give Robb's opponents excellent scoring chances. Robb tries to deflect the puck off to the corners of the rink to avoid setting up his opponents.

● Crease Movements

Coach Mike tells Robb to work on his crease movements, so he begins moving in and out of the crease and back and forth across the front of the goal. He moves from right to left, and in and out, facing shooters from different places on the rink.

Goaltending demands excellent balance and very quick movement. You must be a skilled skater to master the position.

Shooting

Every player wants to get a **hat trick**, which means to score three goals in a game. To do that, a player has to be a good shooter.

● *Wrist Shots*

At practice, the skaters first work on the **wrist shot**. Mike skates directly at the net and shoots from his forehand side. His feet are square, or perpendicular, to the net and his weight is on the skate toward the puck. His stick blade doesn't leave the ice. To supply the power for the shot, Mike snaps his wrists as he releases the shot. Wrist shots are quick and accurate.

● *Backhand Shots*

At the next whistle, it's time to practice backhand shots. Tony approaches the net from a side angle rather than a straight line. He drops the puck to his backhand side, and then rotates his hips, shoulders, and arms in the direction of the shot. The backhand shot isn't as accurate as the wrist shot, but goalies say it's tougher to stop because it's harder to tell where it's going.

● *Snap Shots*

A **snap shot** is more difficult to master than a wrist shot. For the snap shot, Chad's feet are pointed toward the puck rather than the net, with his weight on the back skate. He pushes off his back skate and transfers his weight to his front foot. At the same time, he pushes the puck ahead, creating a gap of about 6 to 10 inches between it and his stick blade. With a rapid snapping motion of Chad's wrists, the stick blade then catches up with the puck and snaps it toward the net.

● *Slap Shots*

Although a **slap shot** isn't as accurate as other shots, it is the fastest, hardest, and most difficult to stop. To execute the slap shot effectively, Mark's weight is on his back skate, the stick blade is drawn back to shoulder height, and his head is over the puck. As he draws the stick through, Mark shifts his weight to his front skate and slaps the puck toward the goal.

As a goaltender, Robb has noticed that the higher the follow-through of the stick, the higher the shot, and the lower the follow-through, the lower the shot.

Passing

To practice forehand passing, the players pair off and face each other, about 15 feet apart. Keeping the puck on their forehand sides, they use their wrists to sweep the puck to their teammates. If you are the player receiving the pass, you should always keep your stick blade on the ice and allow it to give, or move back slightly, as the puck comes to you. Hockey players refer to this as having "soft hands."

To practice their passing, Coach Mike first has the players skate in pairs approximately 15 feet apart around the perimeter of the rink, making short forehand passes to each other. As they begin, Coach Mike reminds them that the person who is to receive the pass should keep his or her stick blade on the ice as a target for the passer.

The players also practice backhand passes. They place the puck on their backhand sides, just as they did for the backhand shot. The pass, however, requires only arm motion and does not include rotation of hips and shoulders.

Coach Mike then has the skaters form three lines at the end of the rink. Marisa enjoys the follow-your-pass drill. She passes to Heather, and then follows the pass by skating into Heather's lane. Heather skates into Marisa's lane and then quickly passes to Marisa. Then Heather follows her own pass and changes lanes. The girls continue all the way up the rink, making as many passes as possible. They finish off the drill with a shot on goal and, sometimes, a rebound.

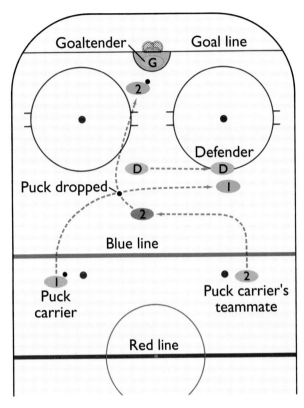

● Drop Pass

Coach Mike also wants his team to use the **drop pass**. In the diagram above, the puck carrier crosses the blue line and then swings parallel to it. A partner also swings parallel to the blue line, staying behind the puck carrier. When the puck carrier is even with the defender, he or she stops the puck but continues skating. If the puck carrier executes the drop pass well, the defender is faked out and continues to skate with him or her. Then the partner can pick up the puck and skate in for a chance to score.

Checking

Coach blows his whistle again, and says "Crunch time!" It's time to work on checks. A check is a method of using one's body to stop an opponent from advancing the puck.

There are two kinds of checks. A **body check** means using your body to bump the player who has the puck so that he or she loses control of it or is hindered from advancing it. A **stick check** means using your stick to steal the puck from an opponent.

Some leagues don't allow body checks. Leagues that do are usually for players at least 13 years old.

● *Shoulder Check*

A check done with the shoulder is called a **shoulder check**. The players line up in pairs facing each other. When the coach says "Now," one player pushes off both skates and drives his or her shoulder into the chest area of the other.

As a checker, imagine a target in the center of your opponent's stomach. This will prevent you from being fooled by a head fake from your opponent. Also, for maximum balance, keep your stick on the ice, your feet wide, and your chin up.

A shoulder check can be used in a *takeout check*. For example, when the puck is passed to Tony, Mark checks him against the boards. He's careful to have his shoulder in front and his leg behind Tony. This way, Mark takes Tony out of the play and comes away with the puck.

● *Lift Check*

Two stick checks are then practiced. The first is the **lift check**. Marisa skates next to Heather, who has the puck, and places her stick shaft under Heather's. With a quick move, Marisa lifts the stick, steals the puck, and skates away!

● *Poke Check*

The **poke check** is used when an attacker is carrying the puck toward the checker. As the checker, Heather skates backward while facing the puck carrier, Marisa. Heather holds the stick with only her top hand, keeping it close to her body. This gives Marisa the idea that there is room to get the puck closer to Heather. This is called the trap. When Marisa enters the trap area, Heather quickly thrusts her stick blade forward and pokes away the puck.

Conditioning

Coach Mike blows his whistle again and tells everyone to skate three laps around the rink at full speed. After that, all the players line up along the boards for the conditioning part of practice.

At the coach's whistle, they all skate forward at full speed across the rink, then stop and immediately sprint back to the starting point. They continue this for two full minutes, until they are out of breath and feel as though they can't continue. Then they have about a minute to allow their heart and breathing rates to return to normal. They do three two-minute bursts, each followed by a one-minute recovery period. This is **anaerobic** conditioning, meaning "without oxygen." Hockey players must condition their hearts and lungs for the intense, one- to two-minute bursts of energy needed in a game.

When the players have recovered, their coach has them again skate forward around the rink. At first they move at half speed, but at the coach's whistle they skate full speed until the second whistle. Then they return to half

speed. Coach Mike continues this for five minutes. This is the **aerobic** portion of their conditioning. In aerobic conditioning you raise your heart and breathing rates but continue exercising. You keep exercising at this high rate for 5 to 30 minutes. This makes your heart and lungs more efficient at supplying blood and oxygen to your body.

The Cooldown

Finally, the coach tells everyone to slow down to quarter speed and skate for another three minutes. This is the cooling or tapering-off part of the session. Its purpose is to prevent muscles from cramping after the hard work.

Coach Mike blows the whistle again and calls all the players together at center ice. He has them stretch while he reviews the workout. The one-hour practice is over already?

Chapter 3

GAME TIME

A hockey team has six players on the ice, unless a player or two is in the penalty box. A team is made up of a **center**, a left **wing**, a right wing, a left **defenseman**, a right defenseman, and a goaltender.

The center is the playmaker on the team and usually leads the attack up the middle of the rink. Wings are usually good shooters who skate up and down the sides of the rink, passing to each other and to the center. Defensemen pass and carry the puck out of their own end of the rink. Their primary purpose is to try to break up the play of the opposing team when it attacks. The goaltender plays with one objective: Keep the puck out of the goal! Technically, goalies can skate anywhere on the rink, but for the most part, goaltenders stay in the goal crease or very close to it.

Ice Breaker!

Manon Rheaume (pronounced Ma-NOH Ray-OME) was the first woman to play professional hockey. She made her National Hockey League debut as a goalie in a Tampa Bay Lightning exhibition game in 1992.

Already skating at the age of three, Manon played in her first hockey game when she was five. She became the first female to play at the Canadian Junior A level and went on to lead the Canadian National Women's Hockey Team to the 1992 World Championship title.

"I didn't try to be the first woman to do this," Manon said. "I do it because I love hockey." After her NHL debut, Manon went on to play for the Atlanta Knights and the Las Vegas Thunder—professional minor-league teams.

Two wings and a center make up a **line**. Defensemen play in pairs. A team usually consists of four lines, three defensive pairs, and two goaltenders. Because fast skating is so tiring, the players on a line and the defensemen usually skate only 60 to 90 seconds before being replaced by fresh players. A goaltender, however, generally plays the entire game.

Face-offs and Penalties

Each period of a game begins with a face-off at the center face-off circle. Players line up on their team's side of the line. An official drops the puck between the two centers, who each try to control it for their team.

Face-offs are also used to resume play after a goal is scored or **offside** or **icing** violations have been called. A face-off is also called when the puck has been hit out of the rink. Where these face-offs are held depends on where and why play was stopped. Offside is called when a player enters his or her team's attacking zone before the puck does. Icing occurs when a player shoots the puck from his or her half of the rink all the way down the ice, so it crosses the other team's goal line before another player can touch it.

For other violations, a player will be given a **penalty** and sent to the penalty box. If a player is given a minor penalty, he or she must stay in the penalty box for two minutes or until the other team scores. For major penalties, the player must stay in the penalty box for a full five minutes, even if the other team scores.

When a player is in the penalty box, his or her team plays **shorthanded,** or with fewer than six players. More than one player from a team can be in the penalty box at one time, but a team must have at least three skaters on the ice. A team that is shorthanded is said to be "killing a penalty." **Penalty-killing** usually calls for a special strategy, and icing is legal for a team that is playing shorthanded.

When a team's opponent is shorthanded, the team with more players is on the **power play.** Teams have specific plays for when they are on the power play, and, sometimes, specific players to carry out the plays.

Officiating

A **referee** is the chief official at a hockey game. The referee, who has to skate as well as the players, is in charge of the game and calls all the penalties. **Linesmen,** who also skate, watch for offside and icing, and drop the puck for face-offs. Off the ice, a scorekeeper-time-keeper records goals, keeps track of players in the penalty boxes, and operates a clock and scoreboard. A **goal judge** at each goal decides when a goal has been scored. If there are no goal judges, the referee must decide.

For games at the beginning or recreational level, two on-ice officials usually act as a combination of referees and linesmen. As referees they call penalties, and as linesmen they also watch for other line infractions.

Because the game is faster at the high school, Junior, college, Olympic, and professional levels, a third on-ice official is usually added.

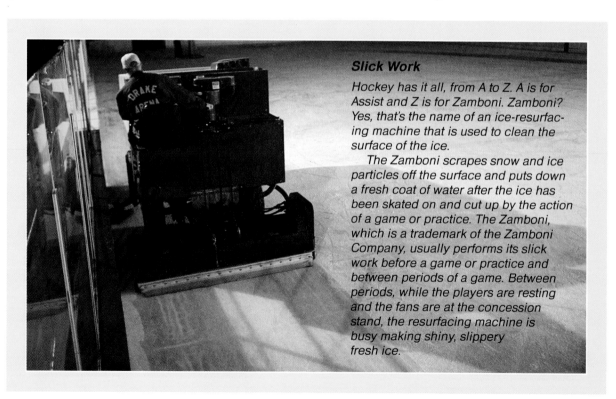

Slick Work

Hockey has it all, from A to Z. A is for Assist and Z is for Zamboni. Zamboni? Yes, that's the name of an ice-resurfacing machine that is used to clean the surface of the ice.

The Zamboni scrapes snow and ice particles off the surface and puts down a fresh coat of water after the ice has been skated on and cut up by the action of a game or practice. The Zamboni, which is a trademark of the Zamboni Company, usually performs its slick work before a game or practice and between periods of a game. Between periods, while the players are resting and the fans are at the concession stand, the resurfacing machine is busy making shiny, slippery fresh ice.

Playing the Game

Tony and Travis are teammates during the school year, but in the summer they play on different teams in a summer hockey league. Travis is on the Eagles and Tony is on the Rams. They are ready to begin their first play-off game in their summer hockey league. Let's see how they use the skills they have practiced all season in a game.

The Eagles win the opening face-off. Tom skates to the red line and shoots the puck into the Rams' zone. Coach has told the Eagles to start with a **dump and forecheck** attack until they get rid of the jitters. This means that rather than trying to carry the puck into the attacking zone, they will dump or shoot it in. Then they will race the defenders to the puck, check them, and try to score.

Mark leads the **forecheck** and goes to the Rams defenseman who has just gained control of the puck in the right corner. Joe skates to the boards on that side, and Travis, their other linemate, is positioned in front of the net. Both Eagles defensemen skate up and position themselves at the blue line.

The Rams are quick, however. They complete a **breakout pass** and begin their attack up the ice. All three Eagles are caught too deep in the zone, and now the Rams are attacking with three of their forwards coming down on two Eagles defenders. The puck carrier cuts to the middle, and leaves a drop pass for Tony, who fires a quick, low wrist shot from the **slot**. The goaltender is caught off guard. Only 38 seconds have elapsed, and the Rams lead the Eagles 1–0!

As the Rams head toward center ice for the face-off, their coach tells them to stay on the ice. They skate for another 45 seconds and then head for the bench. The three players on the next line all jump over the boards and go right into the play. This type of substitution is called changing **on the fly**.

The pace is fast and the Eagles get several good scoring chances. When the horn sounds at the end of the first period, though, it's still 1–0 in favor of the Rams.

In the locker room, their coach tells the Eagles that they are going to switch from their dump and forecheck attack to a puck control system. Travis likes this because he enjoys the passing and teamwork it employs. Coach says, "Remember now, we don't just throw the puck into their zone and give it back to them. If you come up the ice with the puck and there isn't an opening, turn and come back. Pass it back to our defense—then we'll circle and regroup, and attack again."

Coach also tells them to tighten up their **backcheck**. He reminds them that when backchecking, forwards do not chase the puck carrier, but instead pick up the opposing wings. The puck carrier is left to the defense. "Now, let's get out there and play some smart hockey this period!"

Just 21 seconds into the second period, Travis shoots and hits the goal post, and the puck caroms to the left corner of the rink. He wonders if maybe this just isn't the Eagles' day.

Play continues at a rapid pace. With six minutes left in the period, an Eagles defenseman gets a **breakaway**.

As he skates in alone on the Rams goaltender, he is tripped by an opposing player. The Rams player is given a two-minute minor penalty for tripping and goes to the penalty box. Now the Eagles are on the power play while the Rams are one player short.

As they line up to the right of the Rams' net for the face-off, Mark, Joe, and Travis go back out on the ice. Larry and Darrin join them on defense to complete the Eagles' power play unit. Their coach reminds all five skaters to use good shot selection, shooting only from the best scoring angles.

The Rams win the face-off and shoot

the puck the length of the ice. Icing is not called since the Rams are killing a penalty. Precious seconds tick off the clock as the Eagles come back to pick up the puck.

Darrin starts the power-play rush up the ice. At center ice he passes to Travis, who carries the puck into the right corner of the attacking zone. Mark is behind the net, so Travis passes to him and then breaks for the goal crease, calling for a return pass. A Rams defender moves quickly to follow Travis to the net, leaving an open area on the right side. Darrin skates from the blue line into the open ice and Mark feeds him a near-perfect pass. Darrin's shot hits the upper right corner of the net. It's a tie game! Darrin's

teammates congratulate him as they skate to the bench.

The second period ends with the score tied at 1–1. But the Eagles had more shots on goal than the Rams, outshooting them 9–3. In the locker room, the Eagles coach tells them to be patient and to stay with their game plan. And he adds, "Stay out of the penalty box."

The Rams control the opening face-off of the third period and shoot the puck deep into the Eagles' zone. The Rams follow with a very aggressive forecheck, and the Eagles can't clear the puck. The Rams have a new spark. They dominate play until the midpoint of the period, when they get a penalty for having too many players on the ice.

Before they line up for the face-off, Coach calls to the Eagles players, "Let's pick up the tempo and take control of the game again." The Eagles don't score on the two-minute power play, but they do regain the momentum.

Play is fast and exciting for the final four minutes of the game. Both teams get good scoring opportunities. Both goaltenders, however, are up to the task. When the third period ends, the scoreboard reads: Rams 1, Eagles 1.

Because a play-off game can't end in a tie, there will be a five-minute sudden-death overtime period. The game is over as soon as one team scores a goal. That's pressure!

Both teams gather at their benches for a three-minute rest and a few words from their coaches. The Eagles goaltender knows that he'll have to stay up on his skates and cut off the angles to the shooters. For the final two minutes of the rest period he sits on the ice, leaning back on the boards. With his eyes closed, he concentrates on seeing himself moving in the goal crease and stopping the puck.

When the horn sounds to indicate the end of the rest period, the goalie gets up on his skates quickly. The coach reminds the team to forecheck aggressively, steal the puck in the attacking zone, and to take every shot on goal they possibly can.

Throughout the game, the Eagles coach has been matching lines, being careful to keep the Eagles' top line against the Rams' best line. He puts the Eagles' second line out against the Rams' second line. These matchups are good strategy. For the start of the

Playing by the Rules

The rules of hockey are meant to keep the game safe and fair. Some of the more common violations are:

- **Hooking:** *Using your stick to hold another player's arms, stick, or body.*
- **Slashing:** *Swinging your stick at an opponent.*
- **High-Sticking:** *Hitting someone above the waist with your stick, or touching the puck with your stick if the puck is more than 4 feet above the ice.*
- **Spearing:** *Jabbing another skater with the point of the stickblade.*
- **Tripping:** *Using a stick, leg, or skate to cause another player to fall.*
- **Interfering:** *Holding or blocking the path of another player who doesn't have the puck.*
- **Delay of Game:** *Occurs when a player other than a goaltender deliberately freezes the puck with his or her hand or body, or throws or shoots it out of the rink to stop play.*
- **Too Many Players on the Ice:** *Called when a team has more than the allotted number of skaters on the rink.*
- **Checking from Behind:** *Body checking an opponent from behind.*
- **Unsportsmanlike Conduct:** *Swearing, gesturing, or doing anything inappropriate in athletic competition.*
- **Fighting:** *Punching or hitting an opponent. This results in the players having to leave the game.*

A famous comedian once quipped, "I was at a fight and a hockey game broke out." Unfortunately, a few coaches and players have tried to promote rough play, which can lead to injuries and give hockey a bad reputation.

On the positive side, many of the outstanding players in hockey have repeatedly said that fighting does not belong in the game. Violence and hockey don't mix. It's that simple.

Overtime Shooting

While good shot selection is critical to scoring in a regular game, most coaches prefer to have their players shoot more often and with greater abandon during overtime play. The theory is that the opposing goaltender and skaters tend to be more nervous in their defensive zone.

Brad Buetow, a successful college coach, had a simple rule for his players during overtime play: "Don't shoot unless you have the puck." Coach Buetow said it in a humorous way, but the message was serious— shoot often and keep the puck around the other team's net.

overtime, though, he has started the Eagles' second line against the Rams' top unit. It's a bold move, but after 55 seconds, the Rams have had only one shot on goal.

When a high shot goes astray, the puck goes over the plastic boards and into the crowd. The referee blows his whistle and signals for a face-off. The Rams' second line goes onto the ice for the face-off, and the Eagles counter with their top line and defensive pair. The Eagles control play in the Rams' zone and get two shots and a rebound from close to the goal crease.

After the third save, the puck goes behind the Rams' net, and Travis gains control of it. After a fake to his left, he uses a **wraparound shot** to his right, sliding the puck between the goaltender's skate and the goal post. It's in the net! Before Travis can raise his stick, all his teammates pile on him in celebration. The Eagles win, 2–1! The Eagles and Rams meet at center ice to shake hands in the customary rite of good sportsmanship.

Chapter 4

PRACTICE, PRACTICE

Ask fans at any National Hockey League game how they got there, and they'll probably say, "I drove here," or "I took a bus." But ask one of the NHL players how he got to that rink, and he'll have a different answer—"Practice, lots of practice!" Playing hockey well demands highly developed skills, just like music, dance, or painting. The road to the top is paved with hours of practice.

Most coaches like players to practice all the different skills needed in hockey, including skating, puck control and carrying, shooting, passing, checking, conditioning, and team systems.

53

Scooter Drill

Hockey players work on skating every day. At Coach Mike's whistle, the players begin the scooter drill. Pointing their left skates straight ahead, they push repeatedly off their right skates until they are at the other end of the rink. After that, they reverse the drill, pointing the right skate straight ahead and using the left skate to "scoot" or push. This is very good for the power thrust part of skating.

Agility Skating

In this drill, Mark skates forward and does a 360-degree spin at each blue line, being sure to get up on the front of his skate blades as he does this. After several repetitions, he does knee drops at both blue lines. Using his regular stride, he skates forward and drops to both knees and then gets back up as quickly as possible.

Mark also does single knee drops at both blue lines, putting his left knee pad on the ice while gliding on his right skate. The next trip down the ice, he dips and places his right knee pad on the ice and glides on his left skate.

Hockey Stops

Hockey players have to learn to stop quickly and easily. Heather can use the power stop on the front skate. To do this, Heather skates to the blue line and then shifts her weight to her front skate and stops on its inside edge, keeping her knees well bent. Then, at Coach Mike's whistle, she pushes off that same edge and returns to her starting place.

Hockey players also must change directions often in a game. To do this, they use the turning stop. Chad skates to the blue line and stops on the outside edge of his back skate, with his front skate actually off the ice. He brings his front leg back in the reverse direction and completes the turn. The turning stop is more difficult than the power stop, but well worth learning.

Targets in the Goal

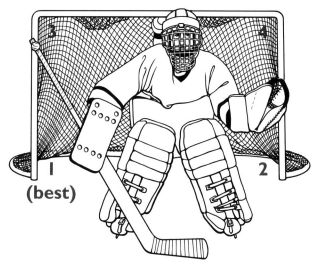

3   **4**

1
(best)   **2**

Percentage Shooting

Hockey players know that the top four percentage areas of the net for scoring goals are the corners. Marisa recalls two general rules on shooting angles:

1. The farther back the goaltender is in the goal, the more room you have at which to shoot.

2. The closer you are to the center of the rink, the better your shooting angle.

Shooting Angles

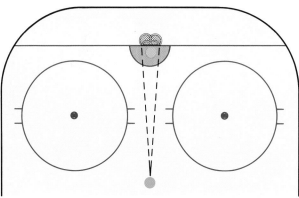

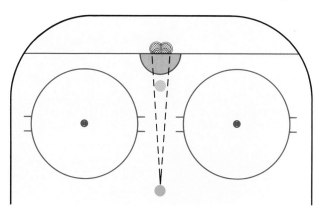

When the goalie is close to the goal, as in the diagram above left, the shooter can shoot to either side of the goalie. When the goalie moves out, as in the diagram above right, the goalie cuts off the shooting room.

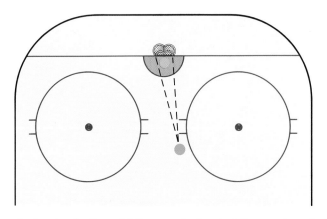

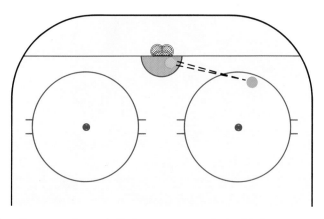

A shooter in the middle area in front of the goal, as in the diagram above left, has more goal at which to shoot than when the shooter moves farther to either side.

The players line up at center ice, and on the whistle one player at a time skates to the top of the circle, shoots, and then goes for the rebound. After several minutes, Coach Mike calls out, "Easy drill."

Starting at center ice, Marisa skates full speed to the blue line, sets her skates at shoulder-width, and then be-gins saying aloud, "Easy Marisa . . . Easy Marisa . . . Easy Marisa . . . ," as she moves closer to the goal. She has her arms out, away from her body, and the puck is at the tip of her stick blade. At about the **hash mark,** she snaps her wrists, flipping the puck into the upper right corner of the net and hitting the "top shelf."

Checking It Out

To practice checking, the players pair off. One player stands along the boards. The other is about two feet away. On the whistle, the players away from the boards execute a takeout check on their partners. After several repetitions, the players switch places. With the same partners, they then practice the shoulder and poke checks. They keep their heads up so that they won't be surprised by a check.

Marisa, Heather, and the other players are tired after practice because they worked hard. But they also had fun. Most of the players got to the rink by getting rides from their parents. They know, however, that they can't be driven or even take a cab to that college, Olympic, or NHL rink that's in their dreams. There's only one way to get there—practice!

Dryland Training

Outdoor ice can be hard to find, and indoor ice is too expensive for an individual player to rent. The good news is that you can practice many of your hockey skills off the ice. This is called dryland training, and you only need to wear shorts, a T-shirt, tennis shoes or in-line skates, and your hockey gloves.

You can practice your stickhandling and shooting on your driveway, garage, basement floor, or on any smooth, hard surface. Regulation or plastic pucks can be used for shooting, and tennis balls, golf balls, or roller pucks are good for stickhandling practice. As you experiment, you will find that you can work on almost all of your shots and stickhandling moves off the ice.

Dryland training can also include jumping rope and running through small obstacle courses that you design.

Home Improvement

A dryland slideboard, like the one pictured below, is a great way to improve your skating stride, and it's easy to build. First, glue countertop material (such as Formica) to a piece of 1-inch thick plywood that is 2 feet wide by 8 feet long. Then, drill holes and fasten two boards, 4 inches wide by 2 inches thick by 2 feet long, near each end of the slideboard.

Next, glue foam padding along the inside edges of the end boards so you won't bruise your feet against them. After spraying the countertop material with silicone spray or baby oil, put on clean athletic socks and you're in business!

Take your hockey stick, get on the board, and begin skating, gliding first to your left and then to your right. Continue alternating sides and you'll soon develop a smooth skating motion. Do this for 10 minutes a day and you'll be pleasantly surprised next season when you get on the ice!

If you jump, spin, turn, and move to your left and right sides rapidly, you will improve your quickness, balance, and agility.

Roller hockey and in-line skating are also good dryland training. You can work on your skating stride, turns, balance, agility, and even puck carrying, stickhandling, and shooting.

Chapter 5

RAZZLE DAZZLE

" . . . He slides off the check and is around the defenseman. He's in alone on goal . . . . He shoots . . . . He sco-o-o-o-ores! The Bruins take a two-goal lead with less than a minute to play."

High school, Junior, college, professional, and, of course, Olympic ice hockey games can all be great sources of learning, especially when you want to focus on more advanced skills. Just ask Mark, Tony, or Heather. But don't interrupt them until it's between periods or the game's over!

Hockey Schools and Camps

Ice hockey can be played in many places, but the most common settings are at neighborhood recreation centers, on club teams, and on school-sponsored teams. If you are looking for a place to get started, or if you already play and want to improve your skills, there are many hockey schools and camps you can attend.

Hockey schools are day settings with on-ice instruction. Camps provide lodging and food, along with swimming, horseback riding, and other activities in addition to ice hockey. Before registering for a hockey school or camp, ask the following questions:

- *How much time is actually spent on the ice each day?*
- *How many players are on the ice during instructional sessions?*
- *How many coaches are on the ice during instructional sessions?*
- *Who are the coaches? Are they adults? Are they actually teachers? If "big name" instructors are listed, are they on location? If so, how often are they on the ice?*
- *Is there a daily curriculum, and what does it include?*
- *What is the total cost?*

Slide-Through and Pickup

Tony especially enjoys watching the local college hockey teams. One of the most effective advanced offensive moves Tony has seen is called the slide-through and pickup.

Coach Mike is helping Tony practice the forehand slide-through. Tony skates toward Coach on his forehand side, with his arms extended and his head dipped in that direction to make the fake convincing.

Tony then slides the puck under Coach Mike's stick, and picks it up on his backhand side. To complete the

Passing Lanes

There are actually two lanes for the slide-through and pickup. One lane (top photo) is the triangle formed by the defender's legs and the ice. It is not quite as effective as the other lane because the defender can move quickly to intercept the puck. The other lane (bottom photo) is under the defender's stick, through the triangle formed by his body, his hockey stick, and the ice.

move, Tony dips his shoulder toward Coach and accelerates around him.

The backhand slide-through is the opposite. Tony fakes to his backhand side, slides the puck to his forehand, and skates quickly around the defender.

Trigger Shooting

Even at an advanced level, only a few of the players can **one-time** a shot effectively. One-timing, or trigger shooting, means to shoot directly off a pass without first stopping the puck. Because you don't delay by stopping the puck, the shot is very quick and often catches the goaltender out of position before he or she can move from the passer's to the shooter's position. Travis can't one-time the puck in a game yet, but he is working on it and is determined that he will have it mastered by next season.

As the puck comes toward Travis, his weight is on his back skate with his knees well bent and his stick ready at shoulder height. When the pass arrives, Travis pushes hard off his back skate and transfers his weight to his front foot. Travis brings his stick blade through in a driving slap shot on the net.

Board-Carom Passing

The **board-carom pass** is an advanced skill, also. In one type of board-carom pass, Mark, the puck carrier, bounces the puck off the boards to a teammate, Chad, who is breaking for it.

Another type of pass, a board-carom pass to oneself, is also done. When you have the puck near the boards and an opposing player is coming toward you, bounce the puck off the boards, skate around the defender, and then pick the puck up yourself.

Checking

Basic checking includes shoulder, poke, and lift checking. Checking range is the area the defender is able to reach with his or her hockey stick. The best puck carriers stay out of this zone until they actually make their move. As in other skill areas, however, there are also more advanced checking techniques.

● *Sweep Checking*

The **sweep check** can be used effectively by forwards and defensemen. As the puck carrier approaches, Mark, the checker, quickly drops to a one-knee skating position. Holding his stick with only his top hand, Mark "sweeps" the shaft in an arc, stealing the puck. This move demands good balance and a quick motion, but it is very effective.

● *Hip Checking*

The **hip check** is probably the most advanced checking skill in ice hockey. It also requires excellent balance and timing. A hip check is used on open ice or along the boards.

As Mark approaches with the puck, Tony sets a trap by giving the illusion that Mark can skate around him on one side or the other. As Mark starts around Tony, Tony bends at the waist and pushes hard off his back skate, driving his hip into Mark. Tony trails his stick in front of him just in case he moves too early and Mark tries to cut back to that side.

Chapter 6

MORE WAYS TO PLAY

Five skaters and a goaltender add up to six on a side for an ice hockey game. Variety, however, makes life interesting, and hockey can be played in many ways. There are four-on-four games with four skaters and a goaltender on each team, and even three-on-three games with three skaters and a goaltender per side. There are checking leagues and no-checking leagues.

Boot hockey is also a popular variation. It can be played on either a regulation rink or on ice without boards. All players wear rubber-soled boots instead of skates. There can be three to six, or even more, players on a side.

Similar to boot hockey, broomball is played with players wearing boots rather than skates. The players use stiff-bristled brooms and a ball, rather than sticks and pucks. The goal frames for broomball are larger than hockey goal frames.

Broomball is popular as an indoor or outdoor sport. Players wear boots and hit a ball with brooms.

Some girls choose to play ringette instead of hockey. The games are similar except for some of the equipment. Ringette players use long, straight sticks to control a doughnut-like puck.

Ringette is played on a regulation hockey rink. Players wear skates and use a stick without a blade to dribble, pass, and shoot a rubber ring. It's fast and fun!

Hockey can also be played on surfaces other than ice. Field hockey is played on grass. Players wear athletic shoes and use short, curved sticks to hit a small, hard rubber ball.

Another favorite variation is floor hockey, which is best suited for a gym floor but can also be played on blacktop or concrete. Players wearing tennis shoes use either plastic or regular hockey sticks to shoot a plastic puck.

Perhaps the most exciting variation of hockey, and one to watch in the future, is the sport of roller hockey. Players wear in-line skates and use regular hockey sticks to stickhandle and shoot a special puck. Roller hockey is most often played on a rink with boards, but it can also be enjoyed on any large blacktop or concrete surface. There are even professional roller hockey teams.

Ice hockey is a wonderful game, and its rapid rate of growth is evidence of its popularity. The many variations of hockey and varying levels of competition allow you to begin playing no matter what your skills and abilities. Explore your options, choose the level that's right for you now, and get started!

Sledge hockey is another version of hockey in which players don't skate.

Sledge Hockey

"Sledge" is another word for sled, and that is just what players use to play sledge hockey. The sport was created in Norway in 1967 for athletes with lower body disabilities.

Sledge hockey teams use six players at a time and play on a standard rink. A regulation hockey net and puck are used. Sledge hockey has rules similar to regular hockey.

Players sit on sleds about three inches off the ice. The sleds have skate blades and the competitors use two sticks with ice picks on the bottom to push themselves around the rink and handle the puck. The goaltenders usually make many saves, keeping the games low-scoring and fun to play and watch.

More teams play sledge hockey every year. A United States team took second place in the World Cup Sledge Hockey Tournament in 1993.

HOCKEY TALK

aerobic: Exercise that helps one's body take in more oxygen and use it more efficiently.

anaerobic: Exercise that helps one's body function in short bursts of intense activity that deplete oxygen stores.

attacking zone: The area of the rink surrounding the opponent's goal, bounded by a blue line and an end of the rink. Also called a team's offensive zone.

backcheck: A system for covering and checking opponents while they are bringing the puck up the ice.

backhand: A shot or pass in which the back of the puck carrier's bottom (power) hand is toward the target.

blue line: One of two 1-foot-wide blue lines that indicate where an offensive zone begins. A blue line is 60 feet from a goal line.

board-carom pass: A pass that is bounced off the boards to a teammate or to oneself.

boards: Sheets of lumber or hard plastic 3½ to 4 feet high that surround the rink.

body check: The act of using one's body to block or hit another player so that the other player loses control of the puck.

breakaway: A play in which the puck carrier faces only the goaltender.

breakout pass: A pass used by a team to move the puck out of its defensive zone.

center: The forward who plays in the center of a line, between the two wings. Centers usually take face-offs.

crossover: A method of skating in which the skater alternates putting one foot across and in front of the other.

deck save: A save by the goaltender in which he or she stretches out flat on the ice on his or her side. Also called a stacked pads slide save.

defending zone: The area of the rink surrounding a team's goal, bounded by a blue line and an end of the rink. A team's defending zone is its opponent's attacking or offensive zone.

defenseman: One of two players on the ice whose primary responsibility is to help the goaltender protect their team's goal.

drop pass: A pass in which the puck carrier leaves the puck for a teammate trailing behind him or her.

dump and forecheck: An offensive plan in which the attacking team shoots the puck into its offensive zone and forechecks aggressively.

face-off: The act of dropping the puck between two opposing players to start or resume play. A face-off is held to start each period, after every goal, and after every stoppage of play.

of the rink that is defined by the crossbar and goal posts and the mesh netting stretched between them. Also, the shooting of a puck over the goal line, between the goal posts and underneath the crossbar. Each goal is worth one point.

goal crease: The semicircle in front of the goal. Members of the attacking team aren't allowed in the goal crease unless the puck is in the crease.

goal judge: An official who stands outside the boards and behind the goal and signals when the puck has crossed the goal line.

goal line: A 2-inch-wide red line extending across the rink 10 feet from the end of the rink. The goal is placed in the middle of the goal line with the line at the front of the goalmouth.

goaltender (goalie): The player who stays near his or her team's goal and tries to keep the puck from entering it.

hash mark: One of several short lines around the face-off circles that designate where players should stand before the puck is dropped for a face-off.

hat trick: The scoring of three goals by one person in one game.

hip check: A body check in which the checker uses his or her hip to check the puck carrier.

forecheck: Pressure applied to the defensive team to prevent it from taking the puck out of its zone.

forehand: A shot or pass in which the palm of the puck carrier's bottom (power) hand is toward the target.

glove save: A save in which the goaltender catches the puck with his or her glove hand.

goal: An area 6 feet wide, 4 feet high, and 10 feet from the end

icing: The act of shooting the puck from one's defensive side of the red line so that it crosses the goal line before a player other than the goaltender touches it. A team can legally ice the puck when it is shorthanded. In all other cases, icing results in a face-off in the icing team's defending zone.

lie: The angle between the hockey stick's shaft and blade. The higher the number, the smaller the angle and the easier it is to control the puck close to one's body. The bigger the angle, the easier it is to control the puck farther from one's body.

lift check: A check done by using one's stick to lift an opponent's stick off the ice.

line: An offensive unit of two wings and a center who skate together.

linesman: An official responsible for calling offside and icing.

neutral zone: The area of ice between the blue lines.

offside: A violation of the rules that occurs when an offensive player enters his or her attacking zone before the puck or when a pass crosses a blue line and the red line before being touched by another player.

one-time: A method of shooting the puck after receiving a pass without stopping the puck first. Also called trigger shooting.

on the fly: A way of substituting players without stopping the game.

pad save: A save in which the goaltender uses his or her pads to stop the puck.

penalty: A punishment for breaking a rule. A minor penalty results in a player being in the penalty box for two minutes or until the other team scores. A major penalty results in a player being in the penalty box for five minutes even if the other team scores. A misconduct penalty results in a player being in the penalty box for 10 minutes but his or her team doesn't have to play shorthanded.

penalty box: A small cubicle where players sit while serving a penalty.

penalty-killing: The defense used when a team is shorthanded because a player or players are in the penalty box and the opposing team is on a power play.

poke check: A check that involves poking the puck away from the puck carrier with one's stick.

power play: The offense used when one's team has more players on the ice because the other team has a player or players in the penalty box.

power skating: A method of skating that involves powerfully pushing off one skate while gliding on the other. Power skating is the preferred method of skating for hockey players.

puck: A 3-inch-across, 1-inch-thick rubber disk.

puck carrying: Controlling the puck with one's stick.

rebound: A bouncing of the puck back into play after the goaltender makes a save and doesn't retain control of the puck.

red line: The 1-foot-wide red line that divides the rink in half.

referee: An official responsible for calling penalties and for the overall control of a game.

referee's crease: A semicircle near the penalty box and scorer's table. When play has stopped and the referee is in the referee's crease, players cannot be in it.

rink: A smooth area of ice. A rink can be inside a building or outside. A typical rink is 200 feet by 85 feet.

save: The prevention of a goal, usually by a goaltender using his or her glove, stick, pad, or skate.

shorthanded: A team with fewer players on the ice than its opponent is said to be playing shorthanded.

shot on goal: A shot that scores a goal or would have scored a goal if another player had not touched it.

shoulder check: A check in which the checking player uses his or her shoulder to bump the puck carrier.

skate save: A save in which the goaltender uses his or her skate to stop the puck.

slap shot: A shot in which the shooter draws back his or her stick to shoulder height before swinging and hitting the puck.

slot: An imaginary triangle defined by the goal and the inside edges of the face-off circles. The slot is considered the best place from which to shoot.

snap shot: A forehand shot in which the shooter hits the puck without first winding up. The shooter snaps his or her wrists to generate the power for the shot.

stick check: The act of using one's stick to take the puck away from an opponent.

stickhandling: Using one's stick to control the puck or steal the puck from an opponent.

stick save: A save in which the goaltender uses his or her stick to stop the puck.

sweep check: Taking the puck away from an opponent by dropping to one knee and sweeping one's stick flat on the ice.

V save: A save in which the goaltender drops to the ice on his or her knees with the knees together and the feet apart. Also called a butterfly save.

wing: A forward who plays on the left or right side.

wraparound shot: A shot in which the shooter starts from behind the goal and pushes the puck around one goal post.

wrist shot: A shot in which the shooter keeps his or her stick on the ice and generates the power for the shot by snapping his or her wrists.

FURTHER READING

Bertagna, Joseph. *Goaltending, A Complete Handbook for Goalies and Coaches.* Cambridge, Mass.: Cosmos Press, Inc., 1976.

Blase, Keith. *The AHAUS Coaches Checking Handbook.* Colorado Springs, Colo.: USA Hockey, Inc., 1986.

Blase, Keith. *The AHAUS Coaches Powerskating Handbook.* Colorado Springs, Colo.: USA Hockey, Inc., 1985.

Blase, Keith. *The AHAUS Coaches Puck Control Handbook.* Colorado Springs, Colo.: USA Hockey, Inc., 1986.

Burggraf, Nancy. *Stick Down Head Up!* Fargo, N.D.: Burggraf Skating Skills, Inc., 3129 9½ Street North, 1992. Training video and manual.

Falla, Jack. *Sports Illustrated Hockey: Learn to Play the Modern Way.* New York: Sports Illustrated Winner's Circle Books (Time, Inc.), 1987.

Foley, Mike. *Hockey, Play by Play.* Wayzata, Minn.: Turtinen Publishing, Inc., 1973.

FOR MORE INFORMATION

Canadian Amateur Hockey Association (CAHA)
16000 James Naismith Drive
Gloucester, Ontario, K1B 5N4
Canada

USA Hockey, Inc.
4965 North 30th Street
Colorado Springs, CO 80911

INDEX